EASY MISSION-STYLE WOODWORKING PROJECTS

Edward F. Worst

DOVER PUBLICATIONS, INC.
Mineola, New York

Bibliographical Note

This Dover edition, first published in 2005, is an unabridged republication of chapters I–III from the enlarged second edition of *Problems in Woodwork*, originally published by The Bruce Publishing Company, Milwaukee, Wisconsin, 1921. All of the diagrams have been reproduced from the original source and have not been altered in any way.

International Standard Book Number: 0-486-44412-0

Manufactured in the United States of America
Dover Publications, Inc., 31 East 2nd Street, Mineola, N.Y. 11501

INTRODUCTION

THIS manual is designed as a guide to manual training teachers who believe that the object of education is the development of the child morally and mentally rather than the acquisition of skill, which so often is made the dominant feature in manual training. Not that the training to acquire skill should be neglected, but it should not be fostered at the expense of the child's broad understanding of nature and nature's laws.

No set of models can express the manual training idea, nor can any definite course of work be applicable to all the diverse conditions to be met with in one city, or even in one school; consequently, the exercises are arranged merely as a basis from which to work.

The fact that a variety of materials is used aids in bringing the work into closer relation with that of the grade teacher.

This relationship tends to instill life into the work of the shop, which should be considered as a school laboratory where the work of the classroom is to be more fully developed.

The emphasis placed on the combination of materials gives a broader view of the subject of manual training. It broadens the child's horizon so that he is capable of appreciating the unusual rather than the more commonplace problems so often imposed on pupils of manual training. The problems suggested are presented in such a way that the trained teacher will have no difficulty to understand their construction. The fact that so much detail is omitted gives the teacher an opportunity to present the detailed operations in his own way, thus making the work more individual.

EDWARD F. WORST.

Chicago, December 17, 1917.

Table of Contents

Problems in Woodwork

CHAPTER I

The Squaring Up Process

The first step in squaring up a piece of stock, is to get something to work from and that is usually a face, or the broadest and longest surface, of the piece of stock. If the piece of stock has been surfaced by machine all that is necessary to do is to take a few fine shavings off the face so that the planer marks may be removed. If this is done carefully and the board has not previously been warped, this is all that is necessary to get the face level. Mark this face with an "x." It is a wise plan not to give a beginner a warped or twisted piece of stock.

The second step is to plane an edge level and square with the face just planed. Mark this edge "x."

The third step is to plane an end square with both the face and edge marked "x." The fourth step is to mark the length with a rule, knife, and try square, and saw off all surplus stock ⅛ in. from this line. Then plane down to this line and square with both the face and edge marked "x." The fifth step is to gauge the width from the edge marked "x" and plane the other edge down to this line square with both the face and the ends marked "x."

The last step is to gauge the thickness from the face marked "x" and plane the other face down to these gauged lines square with all edges and ends. Discourage the use of the pencil.

Solitaire

This game, as shown in No. 1, Fig. 3, is played by one person. Place 32 pegs on sticks, one in each hole, leaving the center hole "A" vacant. Then jump over any peg into an empty hole. Take away the peg which has been jumped. Repeat this operation until but one peg remains. The last jump must land the final peg in hole "A." Any peg may do jumping. Jump in a straight line only backward and forward and right and left. The jump must be over one peg only into an empty hole. All jumps must be made in one straight line.

Nine Men Morris

This game as shown in No. 2, Fig. 3, is played by two persons. Each player has nine pegs. Player A puts a peg in any hole, then player B puts one in any other hole. They alternate turns. Each tries to get as many rows of three as he can, and also to spoil as many of his opponent's rows as he can. The pegs when once set cannot be moved around. The rows may be either vertical, horizontal or on the slant.

The one having the most rows of three wins the game.

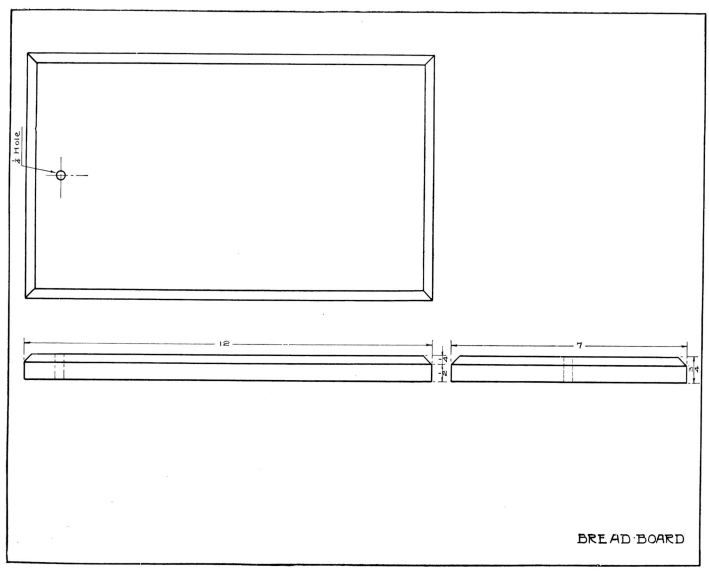

Fig. 1—Working Drawing of Bread Board (Sixth Grade)

10

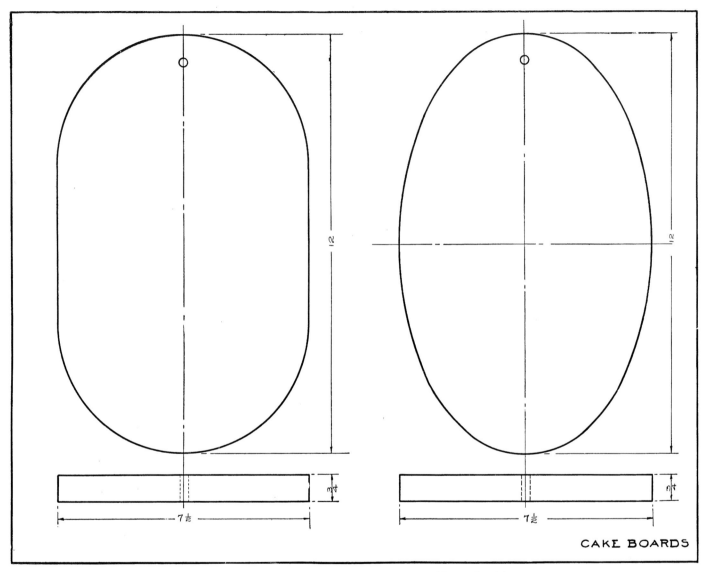

Fig. 2—Working Drawing of Cake Boards (Sixth Grade)

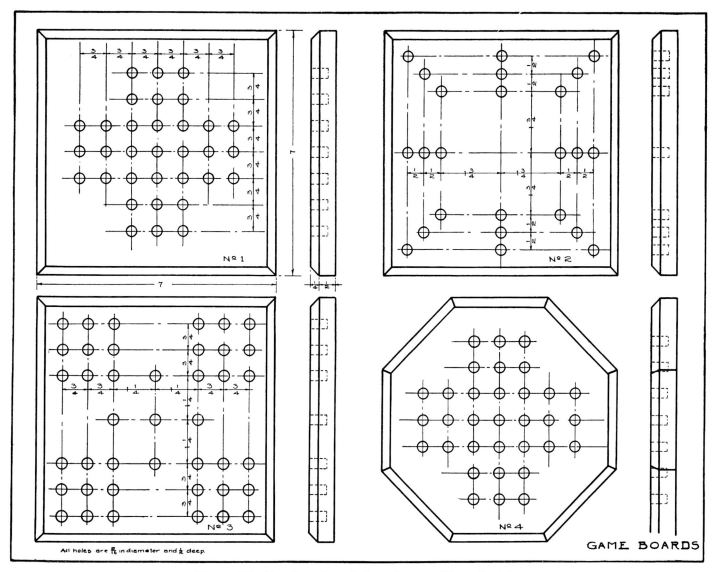

Fig. 3—Working Drawing of Game Boards (Sixth Grade)

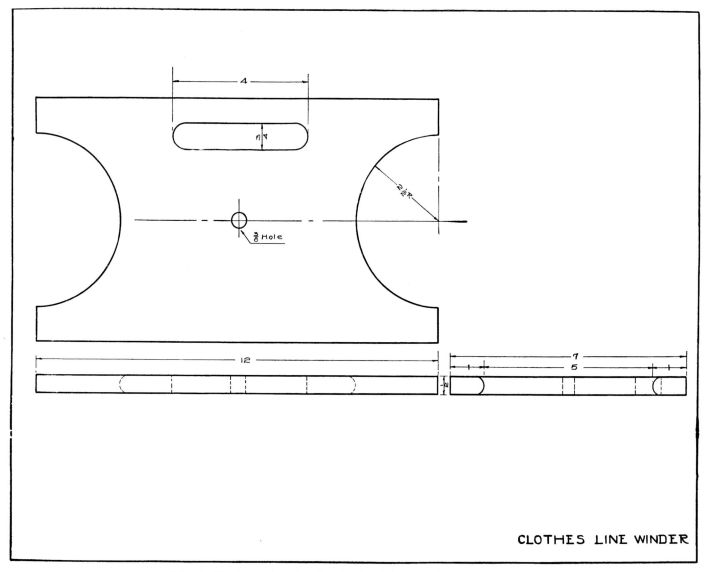

CLOTHES LINE WINDER

Fig. 4—Working Drawing for Clothes Line Winder (Sixth Grade)

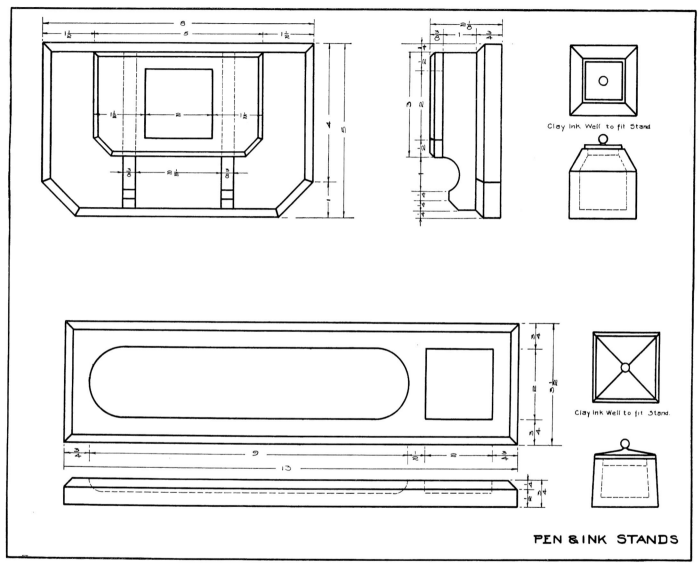

Clay Ink Well to fit Stand

Clay Ink Well to fit Stand.

PEN & INK STANDS

Fig. 5—Working Drawing for Pen and Ink Stands (Sixth Grade)

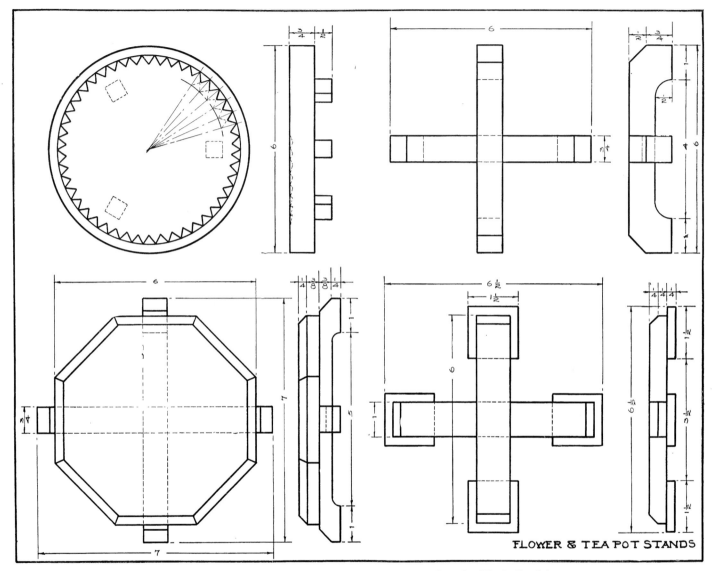

FLOWER & TEA POT STANDS

Fig. 6—Working Drawing of Flower and Tea Pot Stands (Sixth Grade)

Chip Carving

Chip carving, sometimes called "peasant-carving," is the development of the savage's delight in notching with a knife the wooden implements and objects of his daily use. As a home industry it has been most fully developed in Scandinavian countries by the peasants, during the long evenings of winter. As a means for the decoration of objects made by the manual training classes, chip carving has been found very attractive to the pupils and has stimulated them to greater effort in the accurate making of the objects to be decorated, for no piece of work may be ornamented unless it is the product of the pupil's best effort.

There can be no dispute as to the practical value of chip carving in training the hand and eye to deftly use a simple tool, and in showing the artistic effects which may be obtained in the employment of geometrical drawing. The plates on chip-carving suggest appropriate borders for boxes, and tea-pot stands.

Great care should be exercised in designing for chip carving, for ninety per cent of the work done should never be permitted. Avoid using the ordinary star shapes so often seen on boxes, match safes, and tea-pot stands. A simple border, carefully executed, is more attractive than the more elaborate forms. Designs for chip carving should always be carefully drawn with a sharp pencil, the pupils planning their own designs.

This involves an incidental teaching of the most elementary geometry.

Chip carving should be especially interesting to teachers of manual training. The fact that it is essentially a home craft makes it possible to provide profitable and attractive work to be pursued during the boy's leisure hours.

Few tools are necessary. The tool known as the chip-carving knife is all that is needed by beginners.

The work is not fatiguing and may be done on any kind of table, and makes little or no mess or litter.

The numerous objects of home life which may be decorated at a small cost greatly enhance the pleasure of the work.

Fig. 7—Suggestions for Chip Carving Borders.

Fig. 8—Suggestions for Chip Carving Borders

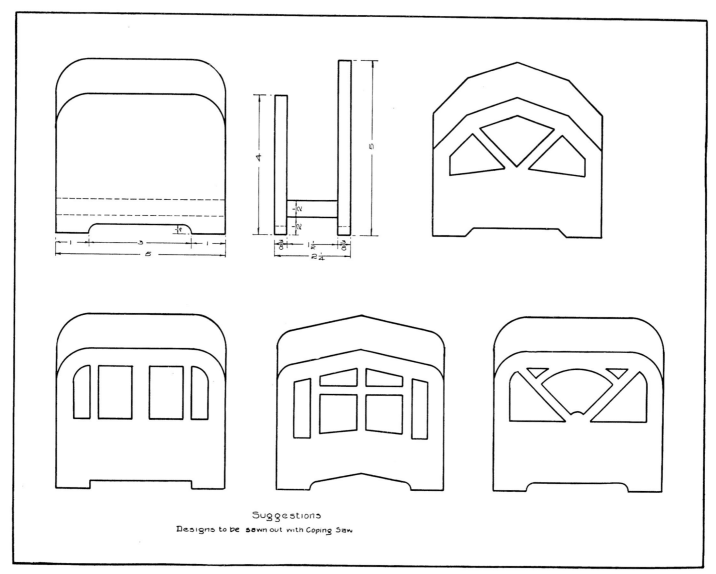

Suggestions
Designs to be sawn out with Coping Saw

Fig. 9—Working Drawing and Suggestions for Designs of Ends of Stationery Holders (Sixth Grade)

Fig. 10—Stationery Holders

Stationery Holders

The stationery holders shown in Fig. 10 are most attractive and simple in construction. Any one of these exercises, as well as the ink stand shown in Fig. 5, gives good practice in construction involving the use of the butt joint. In Fig. 10 the front and back pieces are nailed and glued to the bottom cross piece, the heads of the nails being sunk and the holes filled with filler. The exercise offers most excellent opportunity for applied design. In this case the spaces which may be stenciled are cut away. If stenciling is used the design should be outlined with a sloyd knife. This not only outlines the design but also prevents the color from spreading. Two different colors of stain may be used, or one stain may be used either on the design or the background, leaving the part not stained, natural. Any paint, cut in benzine or turpentine may be used in stenciling. When cut as above described it becomes a stain instead of a paint which destroys the grain of the wood.

A simple chip carved border may be used in outlining the design. If the holder is constructed and left perfectly plain as shown in the figure in the upper left hand corner, a calendar may be tacked or glued to the surface of the front piece, thus breaking up the space and serving a double purpose.

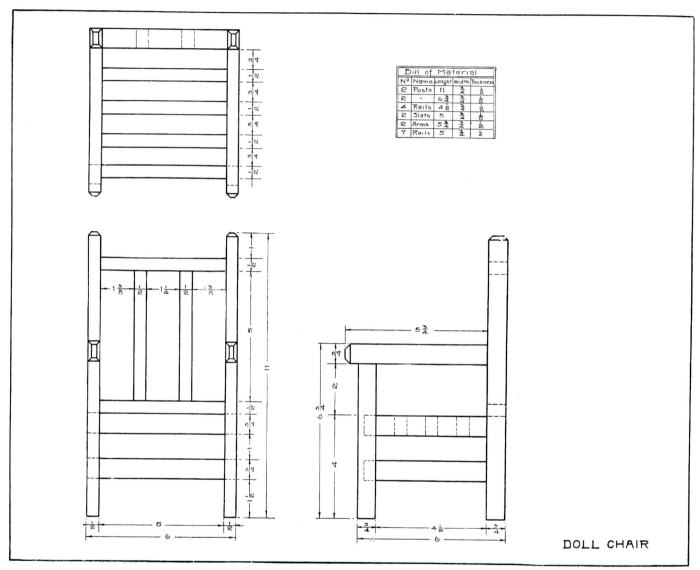

Fig. 11—Working Drawing of Doll Chair (Sixth Grade)

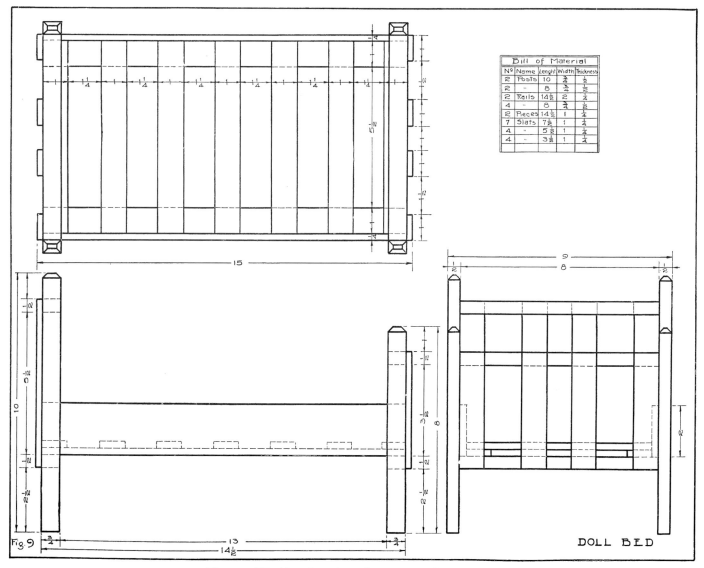

Bill of Material				
Nº	Name	Lenght	Width	Thickness
2	Posts	10	$\frac{3}{4}$	$\frac{1}{2}$
2	"	8	$\frac{3}{4}$	$\frac{1}{2}$
2	Rails	$14\frac{1}{2}$	2	$\frac{1}{4}$
4	"	8	$\frac{3}{4}$	$\frac{1}{8}$
2	Pieces	$14\frac{1}{2}$	1	$\frac{1}{4}$
7	Slats	$7\frac{1}{2}$	1	$\frac{1}{4}$
4	"	$5\frac{1}{2}$	1	$\frac{1}{4}$
4	"	$3\frac{1}{2}$	1	$\frac{1}{4}$

DOLL BED

Fig. 12—Working Drawing of Doll Bed (Sixth Grade)

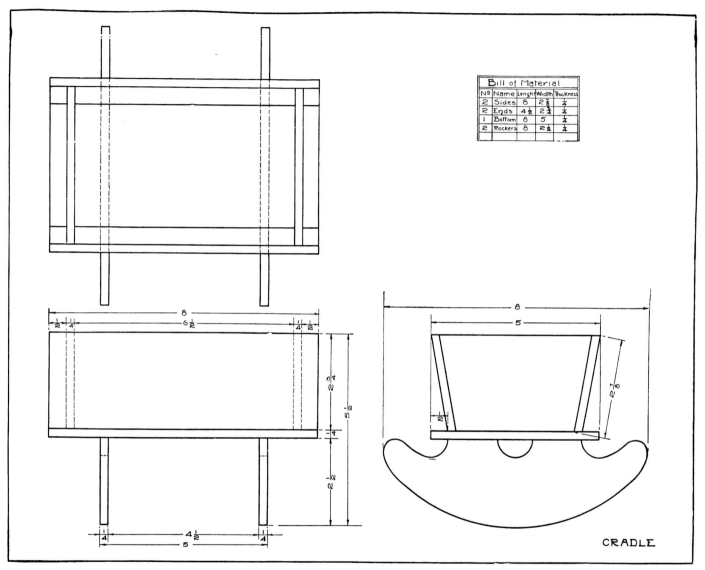

Bill of Material

Nº	Name	Lenght	Width	Thickness
2	Sides	8	2⅜	¼
2	Ends	4½	2¼	¼
1	Bottom	8	5	¼
2	Rockers	8	2½	¼

CRADLE

Fig. 13—Working Drawing of Cradle (Sixth Grade)

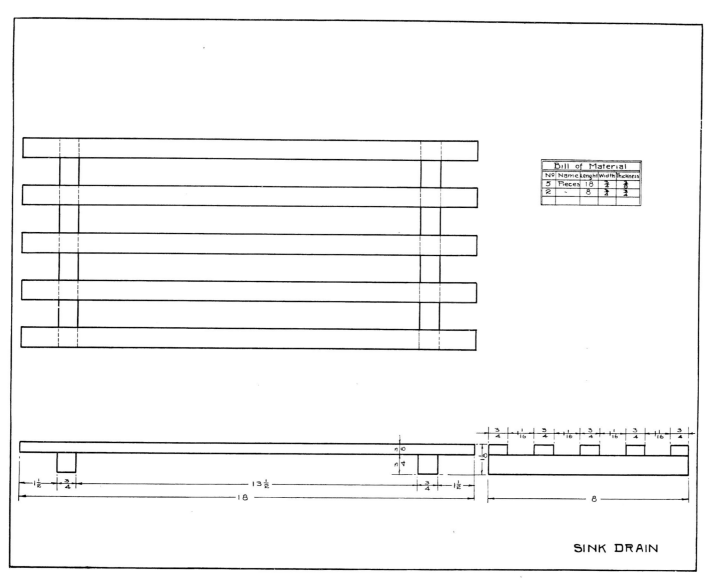

Bill of Material

No	Name	Lenght	Width	Thickness
5	Pieces	18	$\frac{3}{4}$	$\frac{3}{8}$
2	"	8	$\frac{3}{4}$	$\frac{3}{4}$

SINK DRAIN

Fig. 14—Working Drawing of Sink Drain (Sixth Grade)

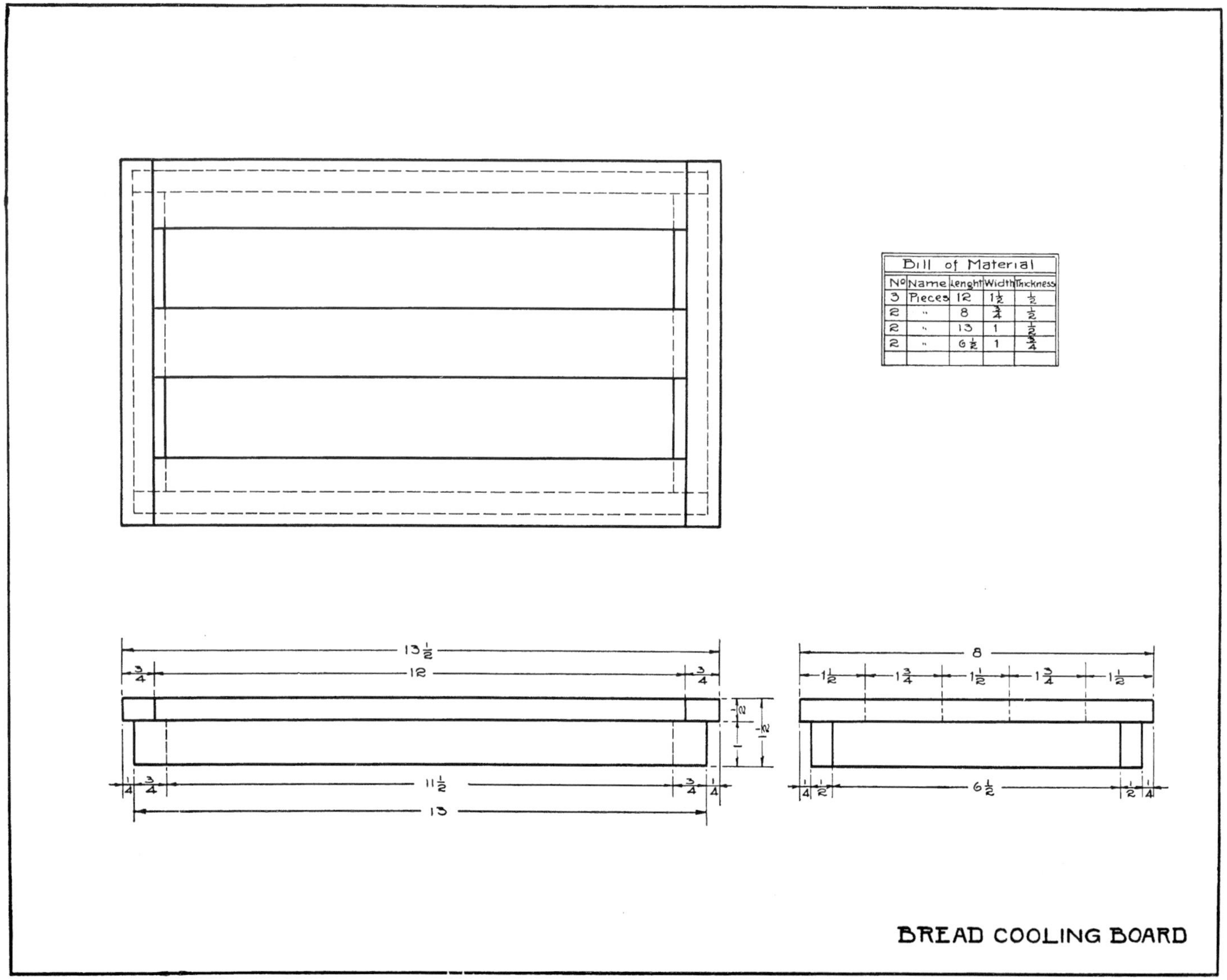
Bill of Material
No Name Lenght Width Thickness
3 Pieces 12 1½ ½
2 " 8 ¾ ½
2 " 13 1 ½
2 " 6½ 1 ¾
13½
12
¾
11½
13
8
1½
1¾
6½
BREAD COOLING BOARD

Fig. 15—Working Drawing of Bread Cooling Board (Sixth Grade)

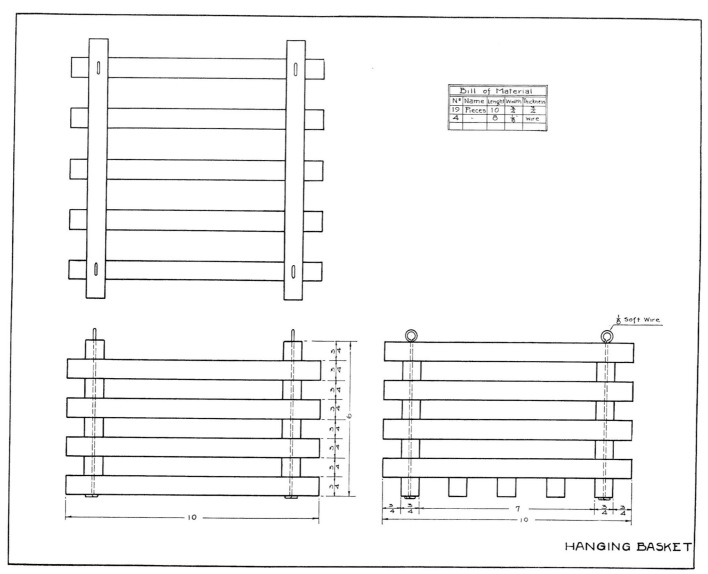

Fig. 16—Working Drawing of Hanging Basket (Sixth Grade)

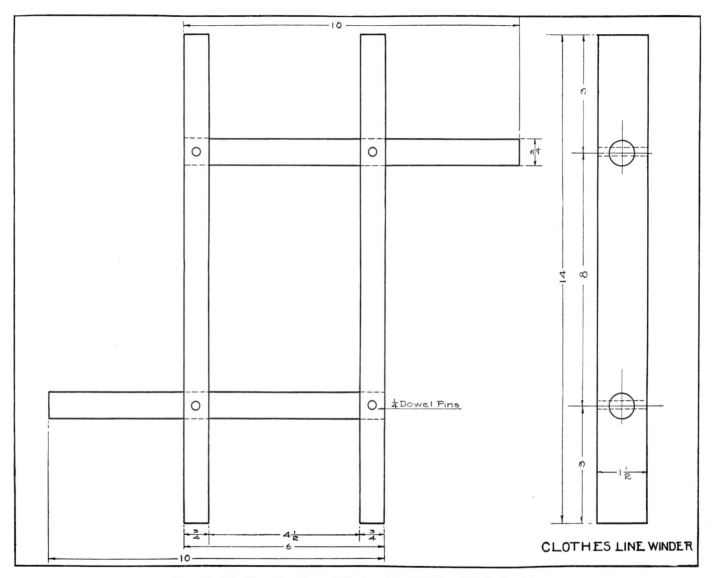

Fig. 17—Working Drawing of Clothes Line Winder (Sixth Grade)

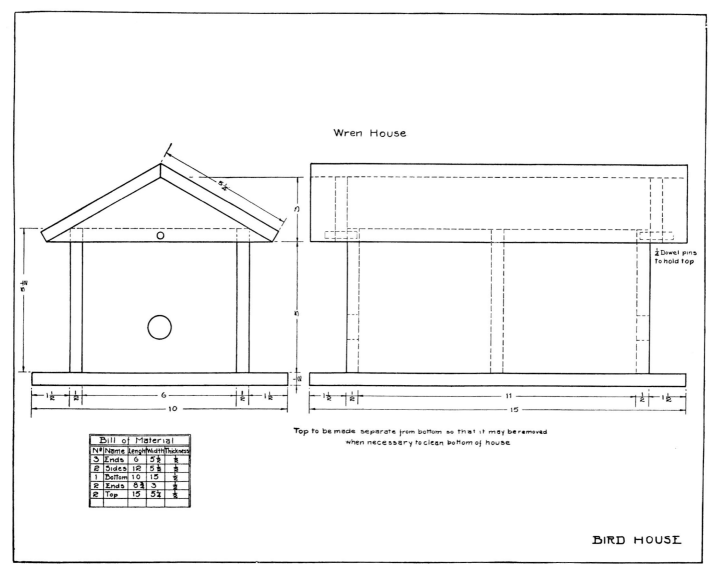

Wren House

Bill of Material

N°	Name	Lenght	Width	Thickness
3	Ends	6	5½	½
2	Sides	12	5½	½
1	Bottom	10	15	½
2	Ends	8½	3	¼
2	Top	15	5½	½

Top to be made separate from bottom so that it may be removed when necessary to clean bottom of house

¼ Dowel pins to hold top

BIRD HOUSE

Fig. 18—Working Drawing of Bird House (Sixth Grade)

Fig. 19—Wren House

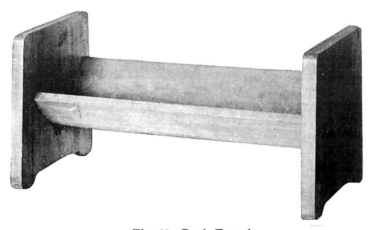

Fig. 20—Book Trough

Bird Houses

The bird life of our nation should be a matter of concern to every one, since the birds are one of our nation's most valuable assets. The loss in the United States to crops, fruits, etc., from insects is estimated to exceed $800,000,000 each year.

Birds are the chief destroyers of insects, and it is the duty, and should be a pleasure, to every man, woman and child to protect these valuable creatures and to encourage them to remain about our homes. The housing and feeding of birds is of national importance. The boys are interested in studying the life and habits of birds and they will do their share toward bird protection. The proper person to help the boys and girls to make houses to attract birds, is the teacher in charge of the shop.

Great care should be exercised in constructing the houses so that they may be conveniently cleaned. The exterior of the house should be kept in the duller colors, as birds are more attracted to this kind of a house. Attention should also be given to the openings through which the birds enter.

If the wren is desired the opening should not exceed a diameter of 1 in., as shown in Figs. 18 and 19. If the opening to a wren house is larger it attracts the English sparrows who are conceded by the United States Government to be destructive to our native song birds.

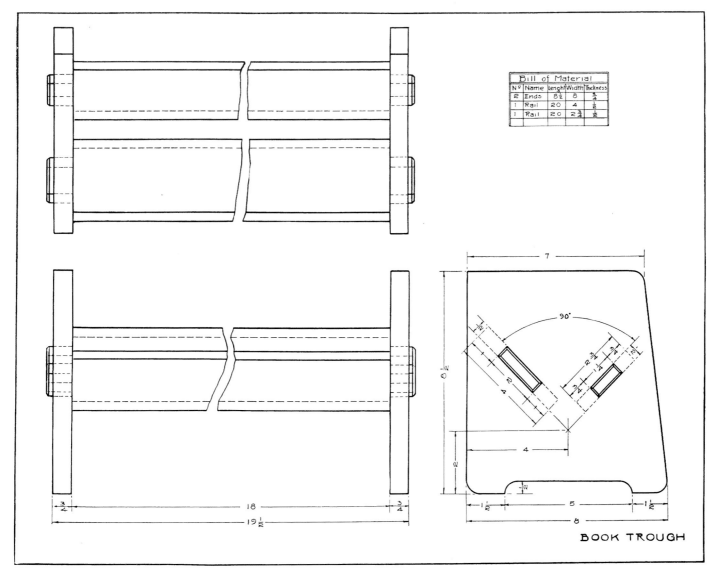

Bill of Material

Nº	Name	Lenght	Width	Thickness
2	Ends	8½	8	¾
1	Rail	20	4	½
1	Rail	20	2¾	½

BOOK TROUGH

Fig. 21—Working Drawing of Book Trough (Seventh Grade)

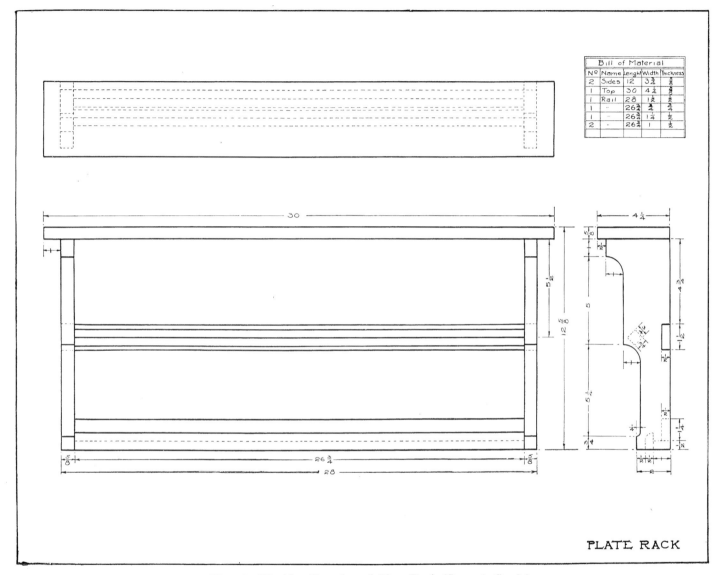

Fig. 22—Working Drawing of Plate Rack (Seventh Grade)

31

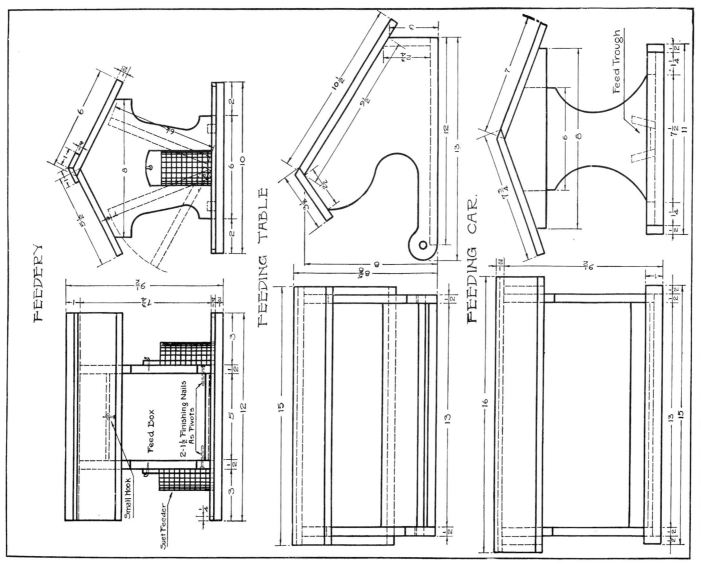

Fig. 23—Working Drawing of Feedery, Feeding Table and Feeding Car (Seventh Grade)

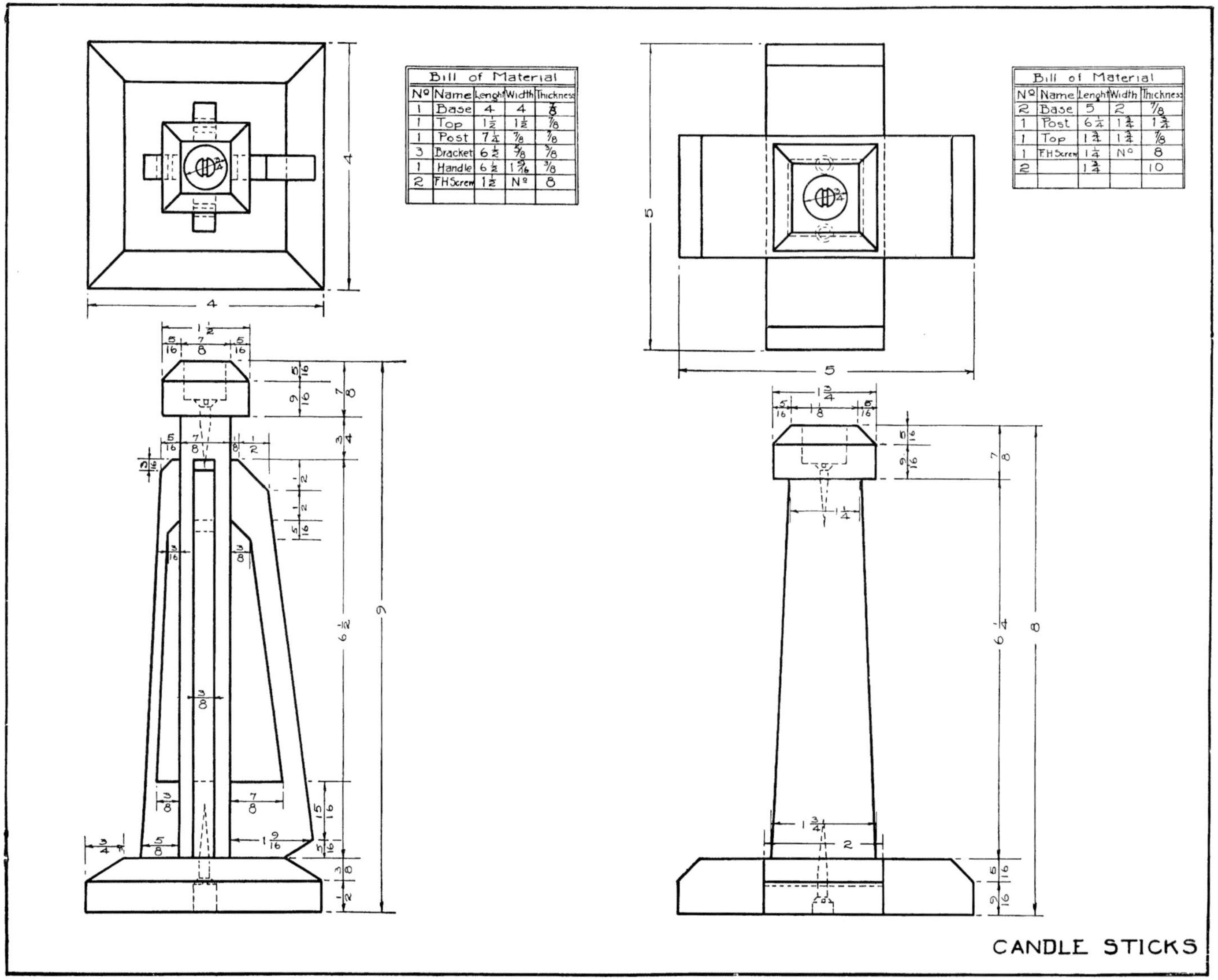

Bill of Material				
Nº	Name	Lenght	Width	Thickness
1	Base	4	4	7/8
1	Top	1 1/2	1 1/2	7/8
1	Post	7 1/4	7/8	7/8
3	Bracket	6 1/2	5/8	3/8
1	Handle	6 1/2	1 9/16	3/8
2	FHScrew	1 1/2	Nº	8

Bill of Material				
Nº	Name	Lenght	Width	Thickness
2	Base	5	2	7/8
1	Post	6 1/4	1 3/4	1 3/4
1	Top	1 3/4	1 3/4	7/8
1	F.H.Screw	1 1/4	Nº	8
2		1 3/4		10

Fig. 24—Working Drawing of Candle Sticks (Seventh Grade)

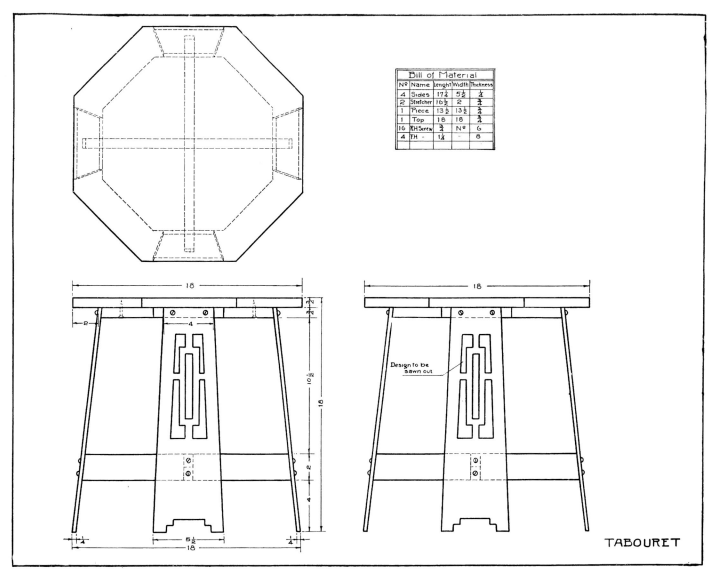

Fig. 25—Working Drawing of Tabouret (Seventh Grade)

Fig. 26—Tabouret

The Tabouret

The tabouret shown in Fig. 26 was made from the working drawing shown in Fig. 25. It is designed to be made in the seventh grade since the construction involves no new joints or operations that are beyond the capabilities of the average seventh-grade boy.

The only new process in the making of this tabouret, that he has not already had, is the gluing up of the two or three pieces of stock that form the top. The gluing up of the top would perhaps be the best operation to do first, for it is the only difficult one in the construction of this tabouret. It might also be a good plan to have the boy dowel the joints of this top piece with two or three $\frac{3}{8}$ in. dowel pins; since it is his first attempt he may not make the joints as well as they might be made, and the dowels will prevent the top from coming apart later.

He may next make the four legs, which will not be very difficult, the stock being $\frac{1}{4}$ in. thick. Then the cross pieces are next required. There is nothing about these that the boy has not already had, for he made half lap joints while in the sixth grade.

The broad or upper cross pieces, which may be made instead of the single piece as shown in the drawing, may now be screwed to the top with $1\frac{1}{4}$ in. number 8 flat head screws, into right position.

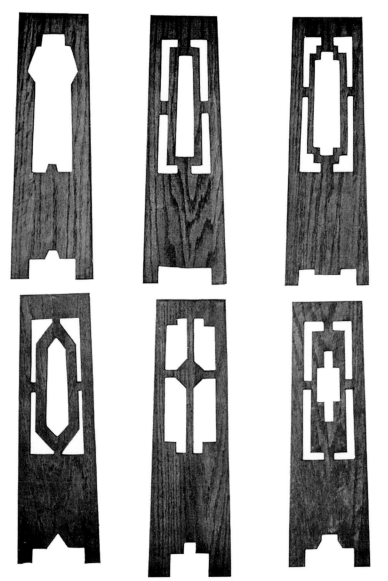

Fig. 27—Designs for Tabouret

The legs are now screwed to the lower cross pieces and then to the upper cross pieces with ¾ in. number 6 round head blued screws. The lower cross piece may be made face up instead of edge up. This would prevent any warping that might occur in the legs, but would weaken the construction.

This is a very attractive as well as a useful piece of furniture when finished, since it may be used as a bed stand, a tea table or a plant stand. The dimensions of the tabouret suit all of these purposes.

Few problems lend themselves more naturally to the applied arts than the tabouret. The pupils study design but fail so often to make application of what they get, to problems of the shop.

Fig. 27 shows a number of most interesting designs for tabourets.

These may be sawed out or they may be stenciled in color, as was suggested for the stationery holders in Fig. 10.

When designing use paper and scissors freely. Through the cutting of paper into various designs, the pupil gets a most excellent idea of the surface covered by his design.

After the cutting, a careful design should be drawn. The drawing is transferred by means of carbon paper.

Every teacher of manual training should aim to introduce as much applied art into his shop problems as possible, taking care that what is used is good art.

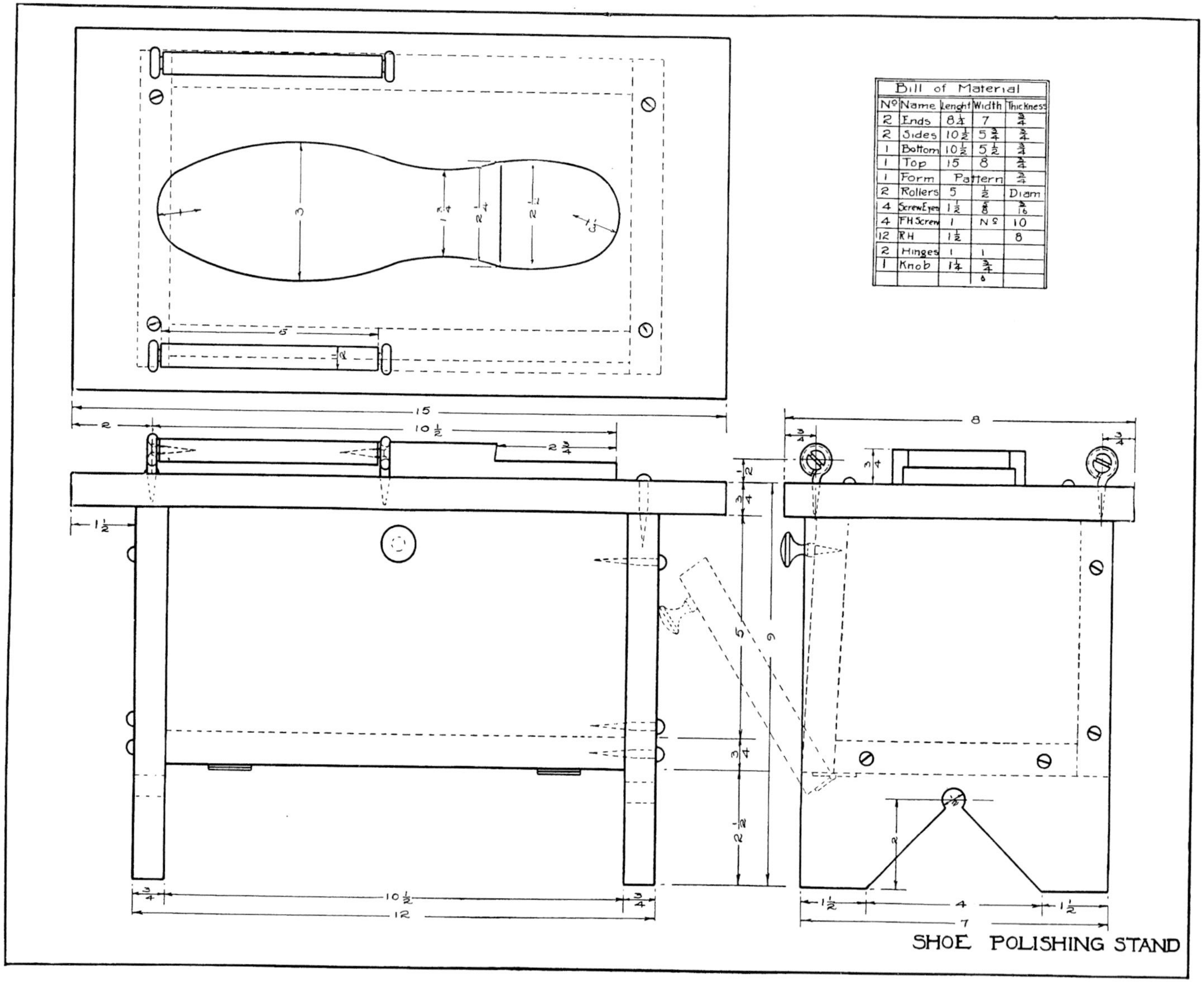

Bill of Material

Nº	Name	Lenght	Width	Thickness
2	Ends	8 1/4	7	3/4
2	Sides	10 1/2	5 3/4	3/4
1	Bottom	10 1/2	5 1/2	3/4
1	Top	15	8	3/4
1	Form	Pattern		3/4
2	Rollers	5	1/2	Diam
4	ScrewEyes	1 1/2	5/8	3/16
4	FH Screw	1	Nº	10
12	RH	1 1/2		8
2	Hinges	1	1	
1	Knob	1 1/4	3/4	

SHOE POLISHING STAND

Fig. 28—Working Drawing of Shoe Polishing Stand (Seventh Grade)

The Shoe Polishing Stand

Fig. 28 shows the working drawing of a unique stand and Fig. 29 shows the completed stand. It is very simple in construction and, though not a very beautiful piece of furniture, it is surely the most useful one that a boy can make. The joints are all butt joints glued and screwed together with 1½ in. number 8 round head blued screws. The operations are the squaring up of duplicate parts and a little spoke shave work in forming the foot rest. The only new operation is the hanging of the door, which is not in this case very difficult. It will be noticed that the door is put on a slant so that it will stay closed without the aid of a catch.

The feature of this shoe polishing stand over all others is the rollers at the sides of the foot rest. A cloth is passed under the rollers and over the toe of the shoe. Then, when one pulls up one end of the cloth with one hand and then the other end of the cloth with the other hand, the cloth passes back and forth across the shoe. With this arrangement one can stand almost erect while polishing one's shoes, while without the rollers one would have to stoop away down.

Fig. 30 shows the working drawing of two sleds, both well within the range of a seventh-grade boy.

In Fig. 31 is shown a working drawing of a community bird house for martins. It contains fourteen separate rooms and is very simple in design and construction. A group of boys might make one for the school yard.

Fig. 29—Shoe Polishing Stand

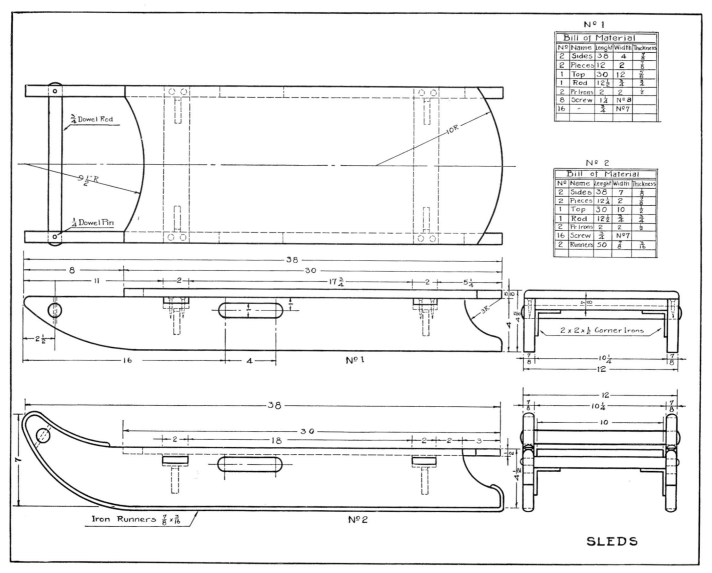

Fig. 30—Working Drawing of Sleds (Seventh Grade)

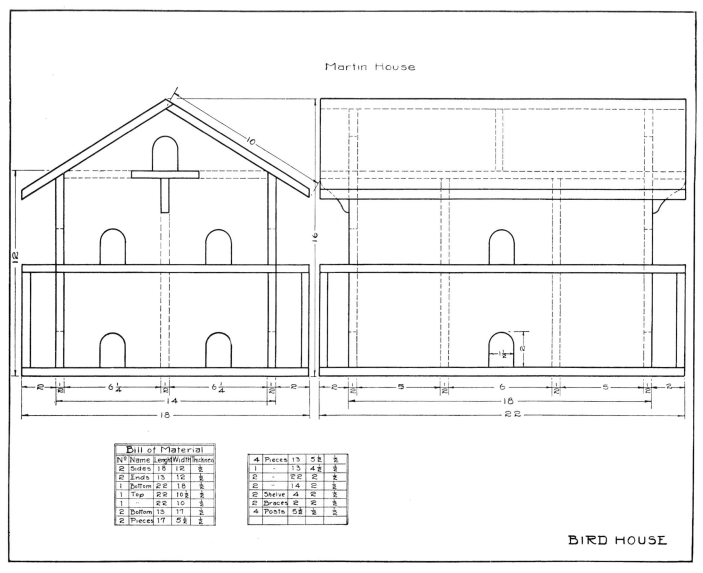

Fig. 31—Working Drawing of Bird House (Seventh Grade)

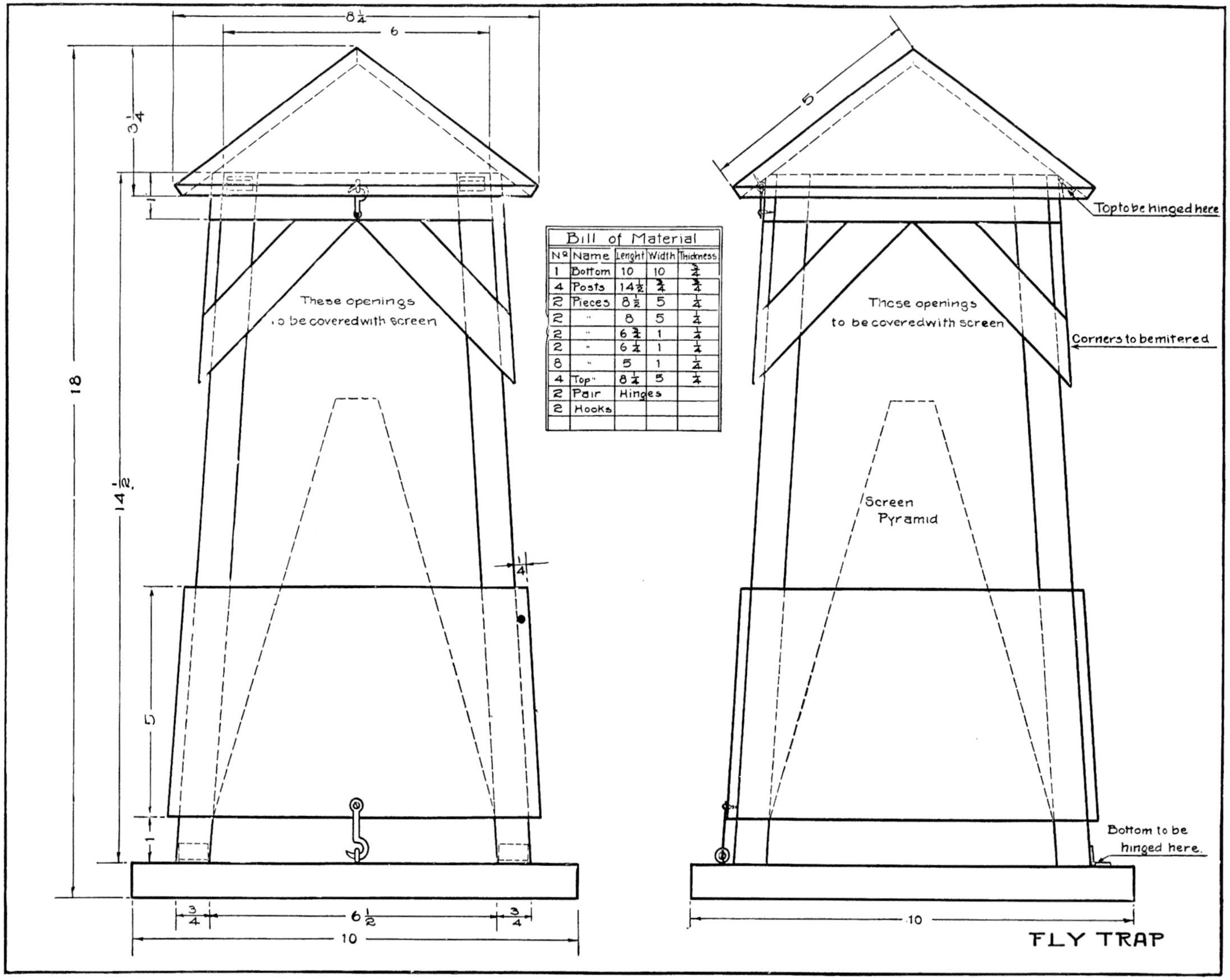

These openings to be covered with screen
These openings to be covered with screen
Screen Pyramid
Top to be hinged here
Corners to be mitered
Bottom to be hinged here.
FLY TRAP

Bill of Material				
Nº	Name	Lenght	Width	Thickness
1	Bottom	10	10	3/4
4	Posts	14 1/2	3/4	3/4
2	Pieces	8 1/2	5	1/4
2	"	8	5	1/4
2	"	6 3/4	1	1/4
2	"	6 1/4	1	1/4
8	"	5	1	1/4
4	Top"	8 1/4	5	1/4
2	Pair	Hinges		
2	Hooks			

Fig. 32—Working Drawing of Fly Trap (Seventh Grade)

41

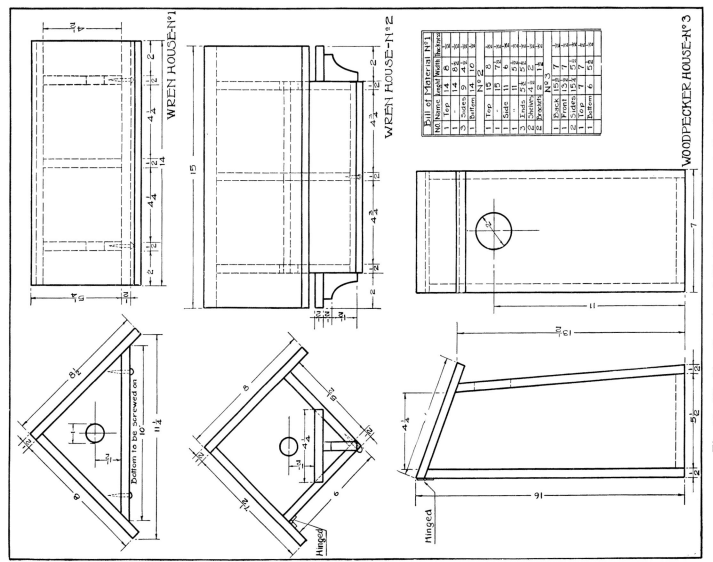

Fig. 33—Working Drawing of Bird Houses (Seventh Grade)

42

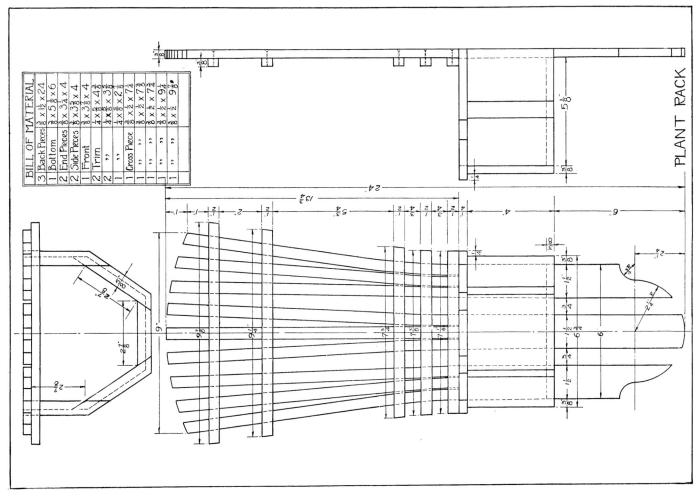

BILL OF MATERIAL		
3 Back Pieces	$\frac{3}{8} \times 1\frac{1}{2} \times 24$	
1 Bottom	$\frac{3}{8} \times 5\frac{1}{8} \times 6$	
2 End Pieces	$\frac{3}{8} \times 3\frac{1}{4} \times 4$	
2 Side Pieces	$\frac{3}{8} \times 3\frac{3}{8} \times 4$	
1 Front	$\frac{3}{8} \times 3\frac{3}{8} \times 4$	
2 Trim	$\frac{1}{4} \times \frac{3}{16} \times 4\frac{3}{8}$	
2 ,,	$\frac{1}{4} \times \frac{3}{16} \times 3\frac{3}{8}$	
1 ,,	$\frac{1}{4} \times \frac{3}{16} \times 2\frac{1}{8}$	
1 Cross Piece	$\frac{3}{8} \times 2 \times 7\frac{1}{4}$	
1 ,,	$\frac{3}{8} \times 2 \times 7\frac{3}{8}$	
1 ,,	$\frac{3}{8} \times 2 \times 7\frac{1}{4}$	
1 ,,	$\frac{3}{8} \times 2\frac{1}{2} \times 9\frac{1}{4}$	
1 ,,	$\frac{3}{8} \times 2 \times 9\frac{3}{8}$	

PLANT RACK

Fig. 34—Working Drawing of Plant Rack (Eighth Grade)

Fig. 35—Plant Rack

Plant Rack

The plant rack, as shown in Fig. 35, makes a most interesting problem for the sun porch. It may be constructed of either poplar or bass wood.

The box part may be made square instead of hexagonal, as shown in the drawing, Fig. 34. The former is more easily constructed.

It will be observed that the ladder part at the back is made of three strips. Each strip above the box is divided into three parts by two saw cuts. The several strips are held apart by small wedges while the cross pieces are tacked in place.

The application of the right kind of design adds to the interest of the problem.

44

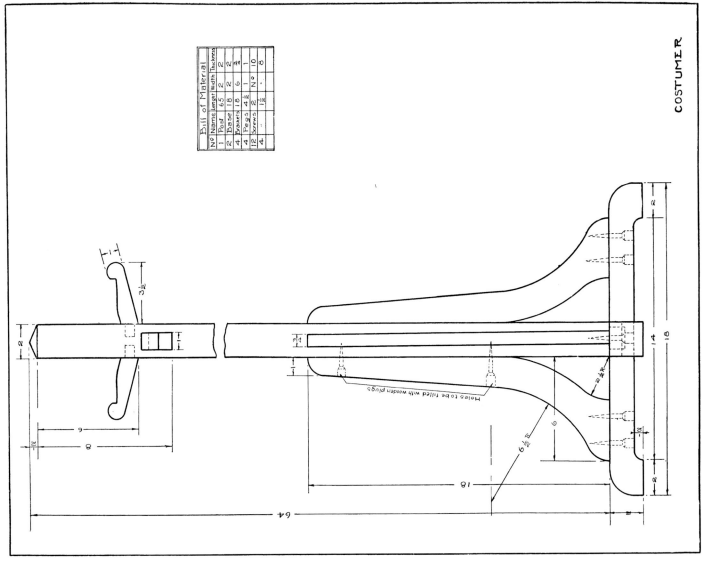

Bill of Material

N°	Name	Lenght	Width	Thickness
1	Post	65	2	2
2	Base	18	2	2
4	Brackets	18	6	$\frac{3}{4}$
4	Pegs	$4\frac{1}{2}$	1	1
12	Screws	2	N°	10
4	..	$1\frac{1}{2}$	·	8

COSTUMER

Fig. 36—Working Drawing of Costumer (Eighth Grade)

The Costumer

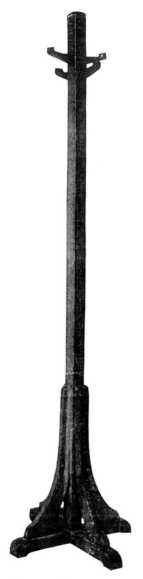

Fig. 37—Costumer

The Costumer shown in Fig. 37 is a very good beginning problem for an eighth-grade boy. It is a large piece of furniture to the boy, and one that he will take great interest in. It is a very useful article when finished, for there is no home in which it cannot find a place, either in the reception hall or bedroom.

It would be best to square up the bottom cross pieces while they are in one piece and then cut them apart to their proper lengths. The bottoms of these cross pieces should be formed before the cross lap joint is made. The tenon should run through the cross pieces and made firm with a wedge.

The braces are next made. A pattern should be made as a preliminary. This can be made of thin wood or heavy paper board. Then the four braces should be marked out on the piece of stock for the same as economically as possible. They should then be sawed out with the turning saw and finished up with the spoke shave and file. There are several methods of fastening the braces to the post and base. They may be nailed with finishing nails, the heads of the nails being sunk and the holes filled with filler. They may be doweled to the post and screwed on to the base, the screws being placed up through the bottom of the base. Or, they may be screwed on as shown in the drawing, the screw heads being sunk and the holes filled with dowel pins or caps.

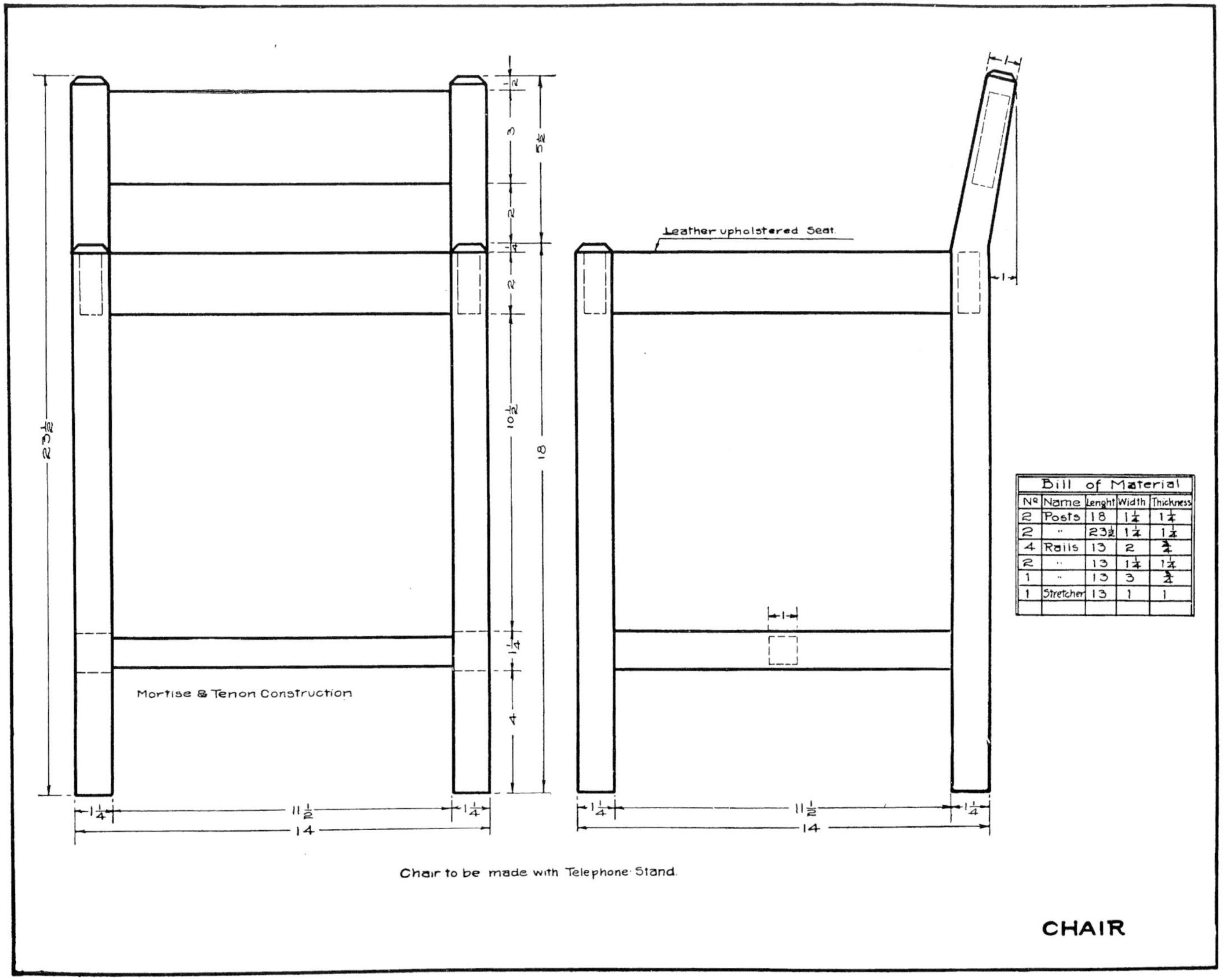
Leather upholstered Seat.
Mortise & Tenon Construction
Chair to be made with Telephone Stand.
CHAIR

Bill of Material				
Nº	Name	Lenght	Width	Thickness
2	Posts	18	1¼	1¼
2	"	23½	1¼	1¼
4	Rails	13	2	¾
2	"	13	1¼	1¼
1	"	13	3	¾
1	Stretcher	13	1	1

Fig. 38—Working Drawing of Chair (Eighth Grade)

Fig. 39—Telephone Chair

Fig. 40—Telephone Table

48

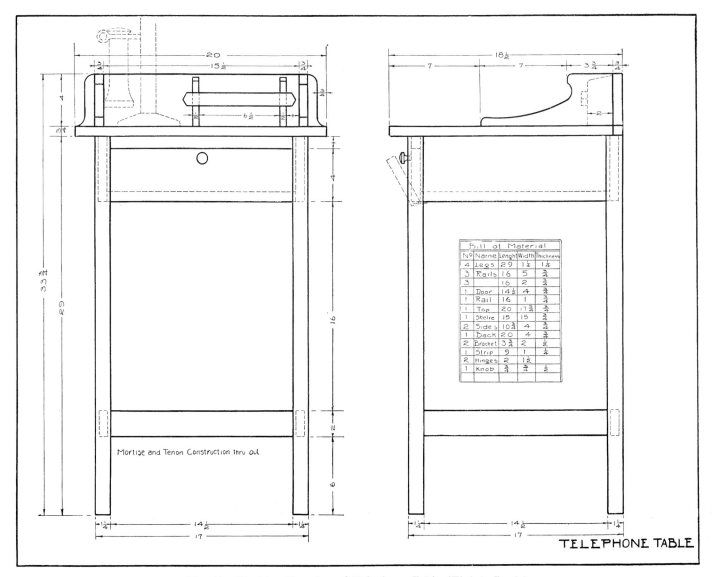

Fig. 41—Working Drawing of Telephone Table (Eighth Grade)

Fig. 42—Telephone Table and Chair

Telephone Table and Chair

In Fig. 42 are shown a telephone table and chair that are surely not to be classed with the ordinary telephone tables and chairs which we find on the market today; and yet there is nothing in the construction of either this table or chair that an eighth-grade boy cannot complete.

Fig. 38 gives the working drawing of the chair, and Fig. 39 shows the completed chair. It may be made either with the mortise-and-tenon, or dowel-joint construction. If there is no band saw at hand the back legs of the chair can be made straight; and if there are no facilities for bending the upper back rail, that may be made straight. The seat is of the slip seat construction.

Fig. 40 shows the table made from the working drawing shown in Fig. 41. This may be made either the mortise-and-tenon, dowel, or the butt-and-screwed construction as shown. The screw heads are sunk and wooden caps placed in the holes.

Instead of hanging the unsightly telephone directory on the table, it is placed in a little cabinet which is made by screwing in a bottom and hinging the front rail onto this bottom, as shown in Fig. 41. A place is provided on the top of the table for the telephone and next to it a place for a pad of paper.

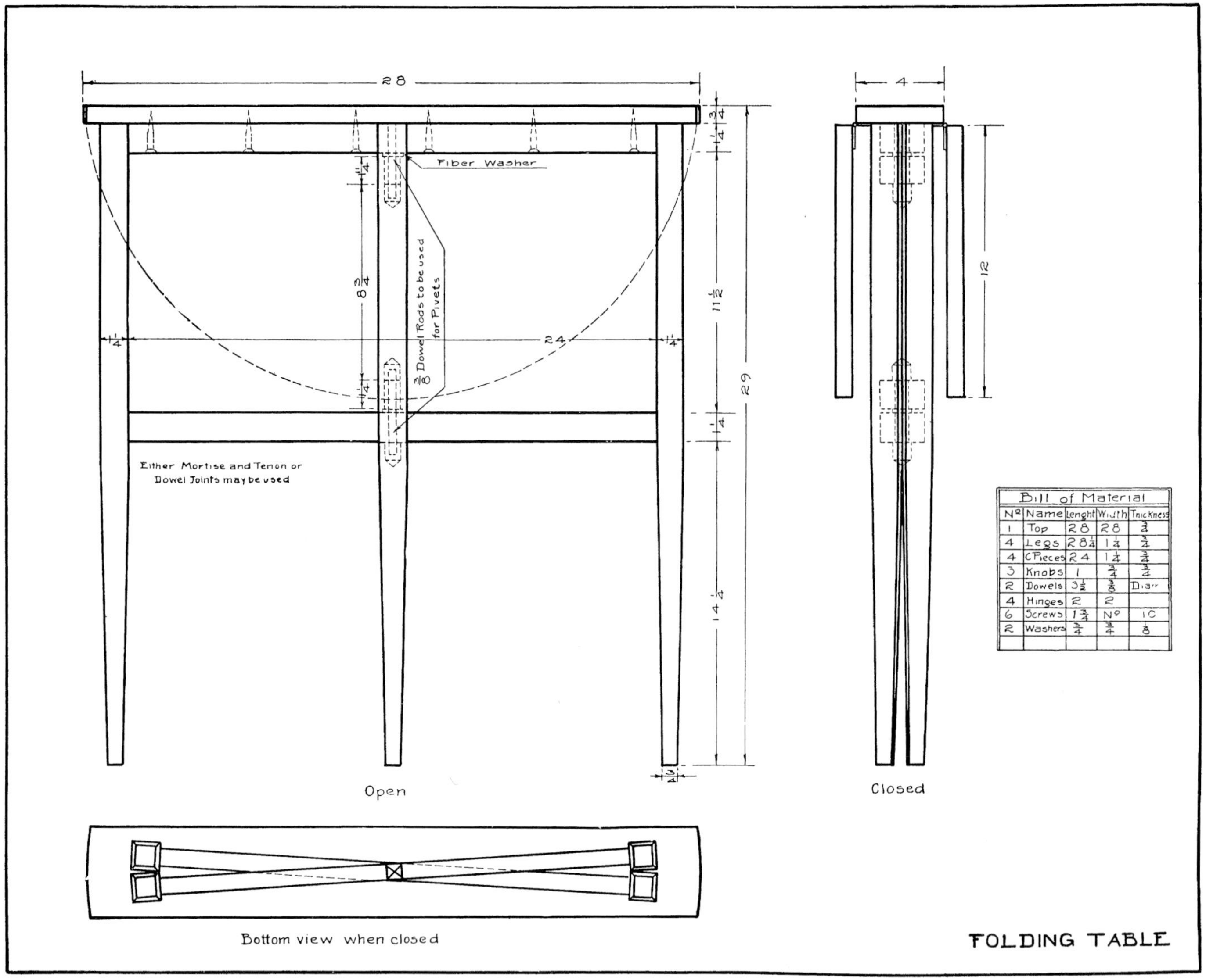
28
Fiber Washer
$\frac{3}{8}$ Dowel Rods to be used for Pivets
$8\frac{3}{4}$
24
$1\frac{1}{4}$
$11\frac{1}{2}$
29
$14\frac{1}{4}$
Either Mortise and Tenon or Dowel Joints may be used
Open
4
12
Closed
Bottom view when closed
FOLDING TABLE
Bill of Material
Nº	Name	Lenght	Width	Thickness
1	Top	28	28	$\frac{3}{4}$
4	Legs	$28\frac{1}{4}$	$1\frac{1}{4}$	$\frac{3}{4}$
4	CPieces	24	$1\frac{1}{4}$	$\frac{3}{4}$
3	Knobs	1	$\frac{3}{4}$	$\frac{3}{4}$
2	Dowels	$3\frac{1}{2}$	$\frac{3}{8}$	Diam
4	Hinges	2	2	
6	Screws	$1\frac{3}{4}$	Nº	10
2	Washers	$\frac{3}{4}$	$\frac{3}{4}$	$\frac{1}{8}$

Fig. 43—Working Drawing of Folding Table (Eighth Grade)

Fig. 44—Folding Table

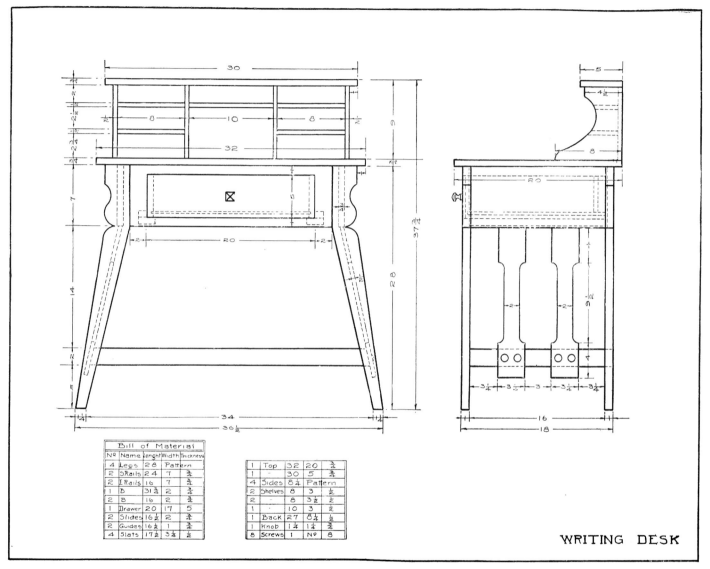

Fig. 45—Working Drawing of Writing Desk (Eighth Grade)

Fig. 46—Writing Desk

The Folding Table

Fig. 43 shows the working drawing of a very simple and useful folding table, and Fig. 44 shows two of these folding tables, one opened and the other closed. The feature of this folding table is its compactness when closed.

The details of construction are shown very clearly in the working drawing. Either the mortise-and-tenon or dowel construction may be used.

The Writing Desk

In Fig. 46 is shown a writing desk constructed on different lines from those of the ordinary type of writing desks. At the first glance it may seem to be beyond the average eighth-grade boy's ability, but when closely analyzed the construction becomes very simple.

To form the different shapes shown one should use a band saw as there is a great deal of form work on this desk which cannot be done very accurately with a turning saw, by an eighth-grade boy.

CHAPTER II

Electric Lamps

Since more and more homes are being equipped with electricity, the making of electric lamps has become more and more popular with the boys in the manual training classes. It is a very good problem for this work, as it allows of a wide range of design and construction. Any of the more common joints may be used, such as the butt, housed, dowel, and mortise-and-tenon joints, the kind of joint used depending upon the grade in which the lamp is to be constructed. Not only does it allow of a wide range for individual design and construction, but it introduces a little of the elementary science work in the way of electric wiring. Here is a chance for the boys to learn the fundamental principles of wiring for electric lights.

Fig. 47 is a working drawing of an electric table lamp which has been worked out and found to be very satisfactory for elementary manual training classes. With the working drawing are a few suggestions for modifying the base of the lamp, showing the unlimited possibilities for individual design. The teacher should have each boy add something original to the design of his lamp.

Heretofore the one real objection to the making of lamps has been the shades. So far the boys who have made lamps have not been able to make shades to go with them to complete the problem, so they had to purchase some cheap, fluffy fabric shades, which, in most cases, spoiled the otherwise artistic effect of the lamps. But now this difficulty can be overcome by the use of the parchment paper in the making of the shades.

Parchment Lamp Shades

There is no lamp shade that is so artistic, lasting and inexpensive as the parchment shade. The parchment is prepared in the manual training shop by the boys themselves from ordinary white detail drawing paper. The wire frames may be made in the shop or purchased at a very small cost. Either water color or oil paints may be used to decorate the shades and these may be purchased at any of the art stores. The paper that is best suited for the parchment is Dietzgen's White Detail Drawing Paper, No. 70. It comes in rolls 36 in. wide and is sold by the yard. Any amount may be purchased.

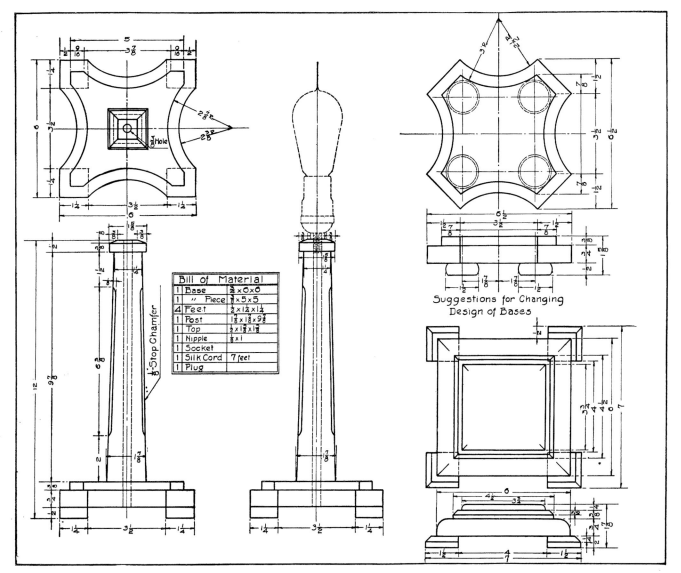

Bill of Material

1	Base	¾ x 6 x 6
1	" Piece	¼ x 5 x 5
4	Feet	½ x 1½ x 1½
1	Post	1⅞ x 1⅞ x 9⅞
1	Top	½ x 1⅞ x 1⅞
1	Nipple	⅜ x 1
1	Socket	
1	Silk Cord	7 feet
1	Plug	

Suggestions for Changing Design of Bases

Fig. 47—Working Drawing of an Electric Table Lamp. (Eighth Grade.)

There are three styles of circular parchment shades, the Empire shape, the cone shape and the Colonial shape. The dimensions for the Empire shape are as follows:

Diameter of Bottom	Diameter of Top	Height
4 inches	2 inches	4 inches
6	4	4½
8	5	6
10	6	6½
12	8	6½
14	10	8¼
16	10	9
18	12	9½
20	12	10½
22	15	11½
24	16	12

The dimension for the cone shape are as follows:

Diameter of Bottom	Diameter of Top	Height
8 inches	4 inches	5 inches
10	5	6
12	6	6½
14	7	7½
16	8	9
18	9	10

The dimensions of the Colonial shape are as follows:

Diameter of Bottom	Diameter of Top	Height
16 inches	4 inches	6 inches
18	4	6
20	4	6
24	4	6

First decide on the shape the shade is to be, and then, from the foregoing tables, select the size best suited for the lamp at hand. When this is decided upon make a mechanical drawing of the shade, as drawn in A, Fig. 50. The shade illustrated is the cone shape, of a size suitable for the lamp shown in Fig. 47. The bottom diameter is 12 in.; the top diameter 6 in., and the height 6½ in. Prolong the sides of the shade until they meet at a common point A, as indicated by the dotted lines in A, Fig. 50. This completes the cone of which the shade is the frustum. Having the completed cone it is easy to lay out the development of the shade. Take the length of an element of the cone, which is a line drawn from any point on the circumference of the base to the apex or top of the cone, in this case 14 in., as a radius and draw the outer circle as shown in B, Fig. 50. Subtract the width of the shade, 7 in., from the length of the element, 14 in., and with the remainder, of 7 in., as a radius, draw the inner circle as indicated in B, Fig. 50. Measure off on the outer circle, B, Fig. 50, the circumference of the base of the cone or shade, in this case 12 x 3-1/7 or approximately 37¾ in., and allowing ¼ in. for lap the entire length

Fig. 48—Boys at Work

to be measured off would be 38 in. Connect these two points A and B with the center point C and the development of the shade is complete. This may be used as a pattern to cut more shades of the same size and shape.

Fitting the Rings

Before applying the design, the rings must be very carefully fitted to the shade. This is done by allowing the two short edges of the shade to overlap. They are held in place by paper clips.

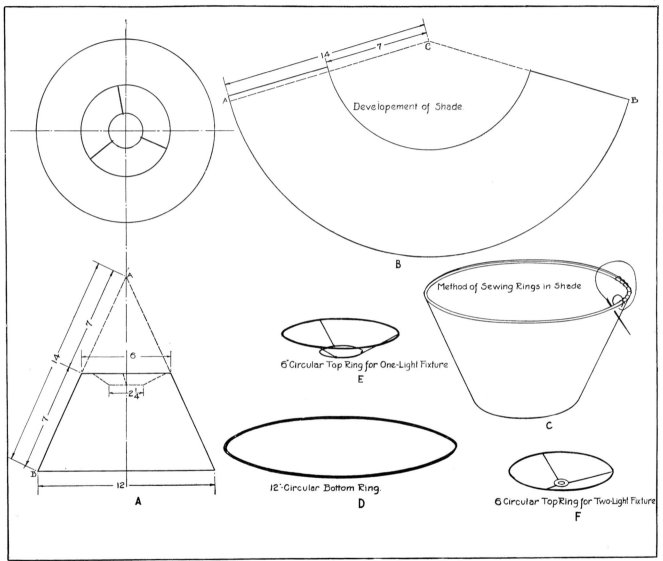

Fig. 50—Working Drawing of Parchment Shade

The boy shown at the left of Fig. 48 is fitting rings to the shade.

After the rings are exactly fitted a light pencil mark is drawn to show the exact place the edges are to come together. An allowance of about ¼ in. is made for glueing.

Painting the Shade

If water colors are to be used, the design is now painted on the shade. When the colors have dried, oil both sides of the shade with boiled linseed oil. After the shade has set for about 15 minutes, wipe off all surplus oil and allow shade to dry for 24 hours. The ends of the shade are now glued together with liquid glue, and the rings sewed in place, using an overcasting stitch, as illustrated in C, Fig. 50. After both rings are sewed in place, a band of braid from ¾ in. to 1 in. in width is sewed over the top and bottom edges to cover over the rings and add a finish to the shade.

If oil colors are to be used the shade is oiled first with the boiled linseed oil, then allowed to dry for 24 hours before the design is painted on.

The lower or bottom rings are always the same in shape, regardless of the size of the shade, D, Fig. 50. The upper rings must be different to meet the different light arrangements. When just one bulb

Fig. 49—Finished Lamps

is used, such as the lamp shown in Fig. 47, the upper ring is made as illustrated in E, Fig. 50, the ring setting directly on the bulb. Where a two or three-light arrangement is used, instead of using a ring to set directly on the bulb a ⅜ in. iron washer is

Fig. 51—Conventional Designs for Parchment Shades

used as indicated in F, Fig. 50, which is fastened onto the top of the fixture.

Designs for Decoration of Shades

The shades may be decorated by using plain, solid color bands, conventional designs of freehand paintings, the amount of decoration depending upon the base of the lamp. If the base is plain, the shade may be elaborately decorated; if the base is moderately decorated, the shade may be decorated with some moderate conventional design; and if the base is elaborately decorated, a very conservative design should be used on the shade.

Fig. 51 consists of a number of conventional designs, adaptable to the parchment shades. The first row are designs based on the butterfly. The top design is of the butterfly almost true to life, the next one is slightly conventionalized, the third is still further conventionalized, and the fourth is purely conventional, so much so that the identity of the butterfly is lost almost entirely.

In a similar manner any object may be taken as a motif and any number of conventional designs made from it.

The second row of designs make most interesting borders. The bottom design shows how the top and bottom bands may be connected by extending the stems from the border to the top band.

The designs may be traced onto the shade and then outlined with waterproof ink. To draw the bands accurately a beam compass should be used.

Electric Lamp

Fig. 53 shows a very attractive little electric lamp, and Fig. 52 shows the working drawing from which it was made. The construction of the post may be a little beyond the ability of the average eighth-grade boy, in which case the design of the post should be changed or modified to come within the boy's capabilities. The rest of the construction of the lamp is very simple.

The wiring of this lamp is very interesting to the boy, besides being very educating To hold the socket, a hole is bored to fit, rather tightly, a $2\frac{1}{2}$ in. piece of $\frac{1}{8}$ in. pipe. The pipe should project out of the top of the post about $\frac{1}{4}$ in. and the socket should be screwed onto this projection.

The wire frame of the lamp shade may be made by the boy, or he can buy it already made at any department store. The stretching and sewing on of the silk, braid, and fringe may be done by the girls in the sewing class of the school. There are no arms or projections necessary to hold the shade to the lamp, as the wire frame is made to set very firmly on the top of the lamp globe.

62

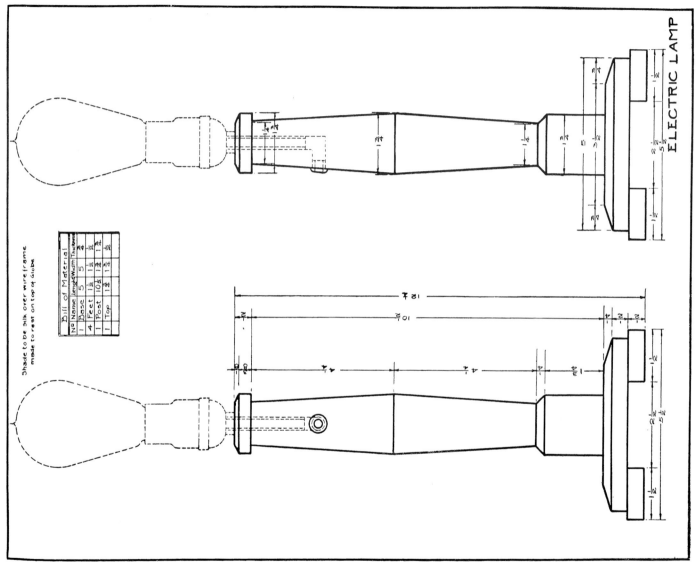

Fig. 52—Working Drawing of Electric Lamp (Eighth Grade)

Fig. 53—Electric Lamp

Fig. 55—Floor Lamp

64

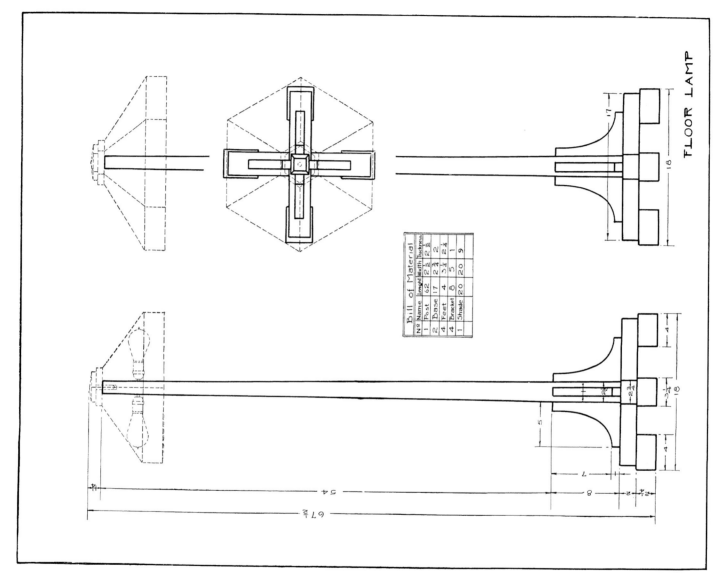

Bill of Material			
Nº	Name	Length	Width	Thickness
1	Post	62	2¼	2¼
2	Base	17	2¼	2
4	Feet	4	5¼	2¼
4	Bracket	8	5	1
1	Shade	20	20	9

FLOOR LAMP

Fig. 54—Working Drawing of Floor Lamp (Eighth Grade)

The Floor Lamp

Since the floor lamp has become a part of the furnishings of the home, we have designed a very simple and inexpensive one, as shown in Fig. 55, which was made from the working drawing shown in Fig. 54, and which any eighth-grade boy can make very easily.

The post tapers from 2½ in. at the base to 1½ in. at the top. It is fastened into the base with a through mortise and tenon joint, and wedged. The braces are then fastened on and, not only do they make the lamp more artistic, but they also make it more solid.

The shade is made of strawboard, and is lined with an inexpensive fabric. A pattern of the sides must first be made, and then the sides may be cut. They are pasted together with strips of bookbinders' cloth, and they are then pasted or tacked to the blocks of wood at the top of the shade, as shown in the drawing. A ½ in. hole is bored in the under side of this block, and a dowel pin is glued into it. A corresponding hole is bored in the center of the top of the post. This is all that is necessary to do to hold the shade on the lamp.

The sockets are placed about 6 in. from the top of the post, and any device may be used to fasten them to it.

CHAPTER III

Metal and Wood

Most teachers of manual training are agreed that flat metal work as a means of decoration has a legitimate place in the shops. The meager equipment required to carry on the work places it within the reach of every shop in charge of teachers who wish to do the work.

Through the introduction of metal, opportunity is given the boy to work in another medium, thus broadening his experience. Among the problems which suggest themselves as being practical are tail hinges, drawer pulls, tray handles, escutcheons, plates for sconces, and an occasional shallow tray to be used with the umbrella rack as shown in Fig. 65, and the smoking stand, Fig. 62 and Fig. 63.

The material and its use create a real necessity for work in design, which should be of vital interest to every teacher of manual training.

In order to design intelligently, it is necessary to know something of the space at our disposal. It is the space which determines whether the applied metal shall be circular, square, or rectangular.

When designing, use paper and scissors freely. The cutting leads to better drawing. When the drawing is completed, it is transferred to the metal. To do this, a piece of carbon paper is placed, black surface down, on the metal to be sawed. The design is placed on the carbon paper and traced. A tracing may be made on rice paper and pasted to the metal. The sawing is done with a metal saw, No. 2 or 3.

The fact that the boys have had experience with the coping saw greatly simplifies the sawing of metal. With a pair of shears and pliers, a saw frame, a drill, metal saw blades No. 2 and 3, a sawing board, and a small clamp with which the board may be clamped to the edge of the table, and a couple of files, very interesing flat metal work may be done.

The trays for umbrella racks require a few blocks which are gauged in such a way as to allow the metal to be shaped in the form of a shallow tray. The exercises suggested in this chapter call for only the most simple work in metal.

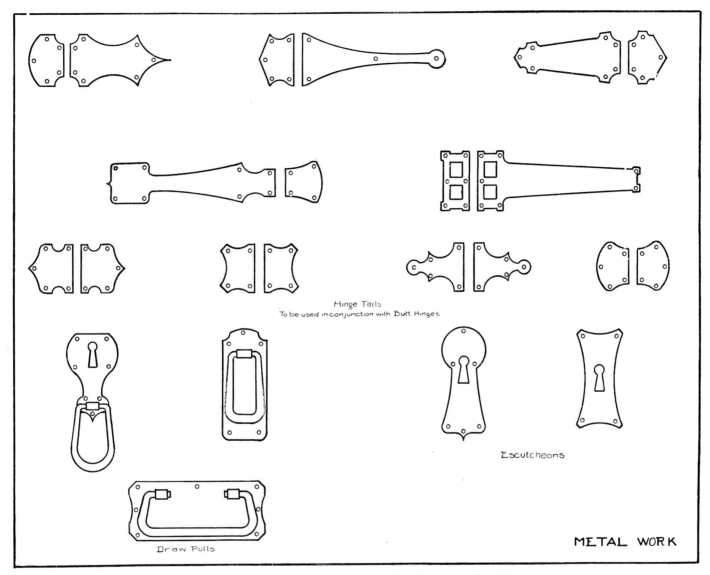

Hinge Tails
To be used in conjunction with Butt Hinges

Escutcheons

Draw Pulls

METAL WORK

Fig. 56——Designs for Work in Metal (Eighth Grade)

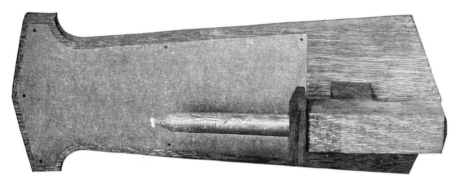

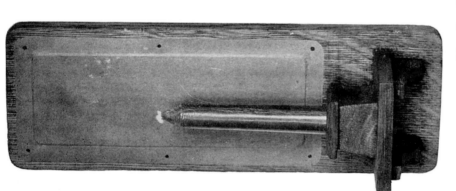

Fig. 57—Candle Sconces

Fig. 58—Stationery Case

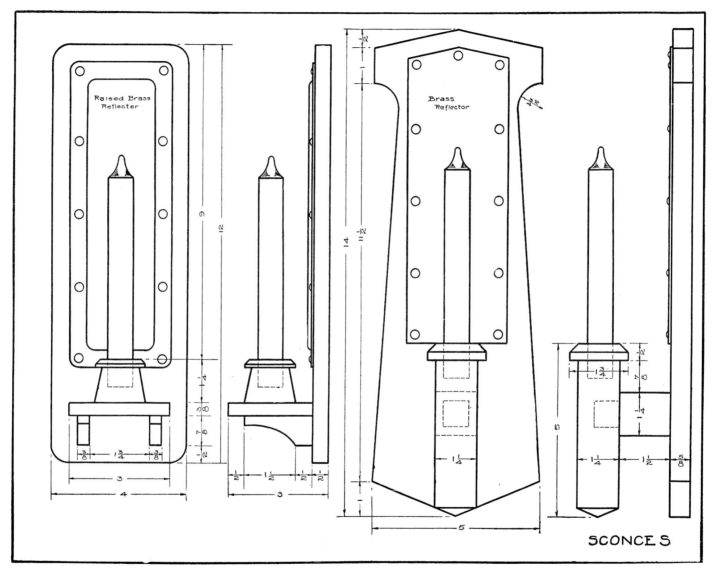

Fig. 59—Working Drawing of Candle Sconces (Seventh Grade)

70

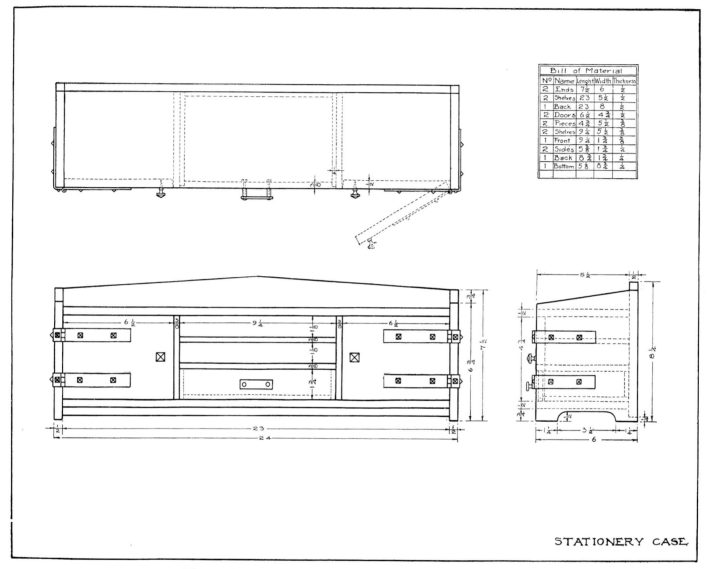

Fig. 60—Working Drawing of Stationery Case (Seventh Grade)

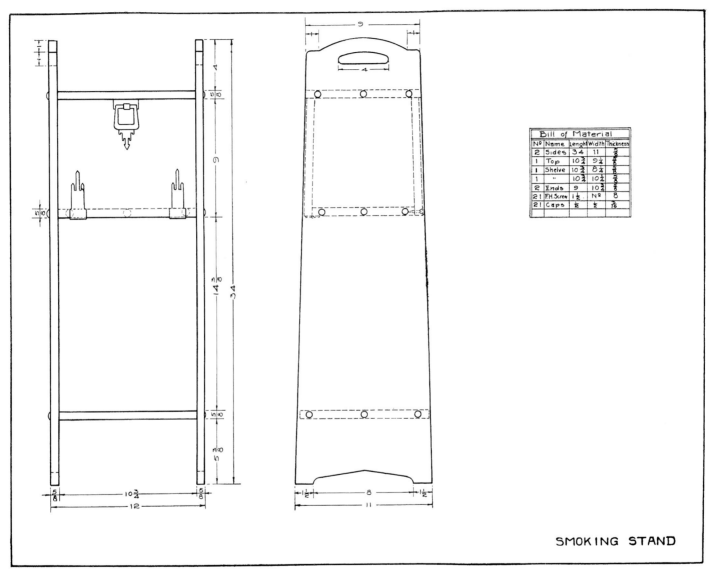

Bill of Material

Nº	Name	Lenght	Width	Thickness
2	Sides	34	11	
1	Top	10½	9½	
1	Shelve	10½	8½	
1	"	10½	10½	
2	Ends	9	10⅞	
21	F.H.Screw	1½	Nº	8
21	Caps	½	½	⅝

SMOKING STAND

Fig. 61—Working Drawing of Smoking Stand (Eighth Grade)

Fig. 62—Smoking Stand

Fig. 63—Smoking Stand

73

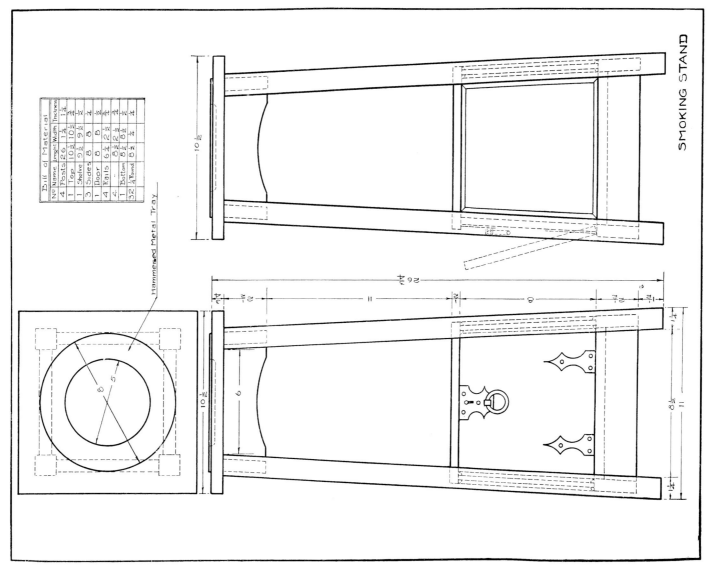

SMOKING STAND

Fig. 64—Working Drawing of Smoking Stand (Eighth Grade)

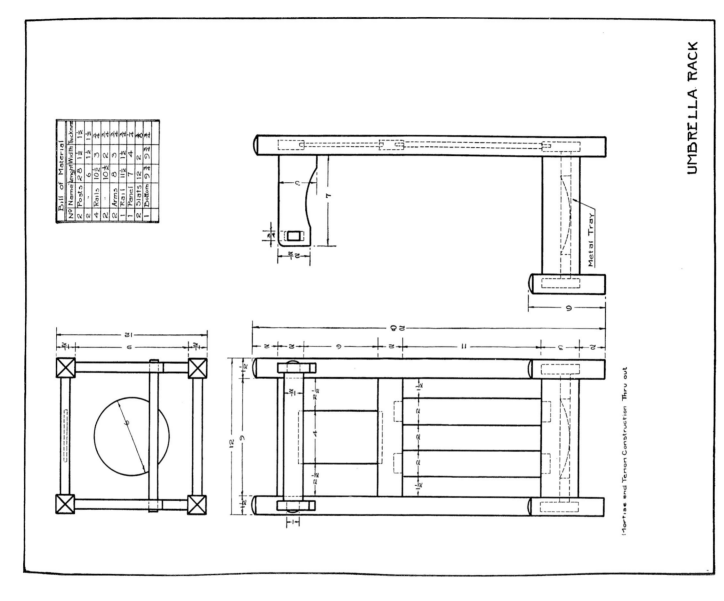

Fig. 65—Working Drawing of Umbrella Rack (Eighth Grade)